Seven Wonders of
GREEN BUILDING
TECHNOLOGY

Karen Sirvaitis

TWENTY-FIRST CENTURY BOOKS

Minneapolis

Twenty-First Century Books
A division of Lerner Publishing Group, Inc.
241 First Avenue North
Minneapolis, MN 55401 U.S.A.

Website address: www.lernerbooks.com

Library of Congress Cataloging-in-Publication Data

Sirvaitis, Karen, 1961–
    Seven wonders of green building technology / by Karen Sirvaitis.
      p.   cm. — (Seven wonders)
    Includes bibliographical references and index.
    ISBN 978-0-7613-4242-7 (lib. bdg. : alk. paper)
    1. Sustainable buildings—Juvenile literature. 2. Sustainable construction—Juvenile literature. I. Title.
  TH880.S58 2010
  720'.47—dc22   2009020317

Manufactured in the United States of America
1 – DP – 12/15/09

Contents

*P*EOPLE LOVE TO MAKE LISTS OF THE BIGGEST AND THE BEST. ALMOST TWENTY-FIVE HUNDRED YEARS AGO, A GREEK WRITER NAMED HERODOTUS MADE A LIST OF THE MOST AWESOME THINGS EVER BUILT BY PEOPLE. THE LIST INCLUDED BUILDINGS, STATUES, AND OTHER OBJECTS THAT WERE LARGE, WONDROUS, AND IMPRESSIVE. LATER, OTHER WRITERS ADDED NEW ITEMS TO THE LIST. WRITERS EVENTUALLY AGREED ON A FINAL LIST. IT WAS CALLED THE SEVEN WONDERS OF THE ANCIENT WORLD.

The list became so famous that people began imitating it. They made other lists of wonders. They listed the Seven Wonders of the Modern World and the Seven Wonders of the Middle Ages. People even made lists of undersea wonders.

Going Green

This book is about the Seven Wonders of Green Building Technology. People often use the word *green* to describe things that are good for nature and the environment. When people stop doing something that pollutes the environment, they say they're "going green." Other terms to describe things that are good for the environment are *Earth friendly*, *eco-friendly*, and *environmentally friendly*.

Technology is another word for tools. People use certain tools, such as bulldozers and cranes, to construct buildings. They use other tools, such as heating, air-conditioning, electrical, and water systems, to keep buildings running. The term *building technology* refers to all the machines and techniques people use to construct and operate buildings.

Some building technology can hurt the environment. Most buildings create pollution by using up a lot of energy and resources. The goal of green building technology is to make buildings and even whole communities that save energy and resources and that work in harmony with the environment.

FANTASY IN GREEN

Imagine a world where, every day, you and everyone else are making a positive difference. In this world, almost everything you use can be recycled, or used again. Things that can't be recycled break down into soil in your backyard compost heap. Your home and school use heating and cooling systems that rely on clean energy—the kind of energy that does not create pollution. Your family's car is made in an eco-friendly factory. It also runs on clean energy.

This scenario is not just a fantasy. In this book, you'll learn about seven green construction projects that are bringing us closer to this kind of world. You'll read about buildings that get their energy from the sun. You'll learn about houses made from recycled materials. You'll learn how people use rain and wind to make buildings cooler, cleaner, and more Earth friendly. These projects are in North America, Europe, and Asia. They show that people all around the world want to create a cleaner environment. Read on to visit this new world of green construction.

Homes like this Earthship are built out of recycled materials.

1 BedZED

People living in BedZED use fewer natural resources than their neighbors. BedZED dwellers use 81 percent less energy to heat their homes, 45 percent less electricity, and 58 percent less water.

$\mathcal{F}$OR PEOPLE WHO LIVE IN BEDZED, PROTECTING THE ENVIRONMENT IS MORE THAN A NICE THOUGHT. IT'S A WAY OF LIFE. BEDZED IS A LARGE HOUSING DEVELOPMENT IN THE UNITED KINGDOM. BED STANDS FOR BEDDINGTON, THE AREA WHERE THE DEVELOPMENT IS LOCATED. ZED STANDS FOR ZERO ENERGY DEVELOPMENT.

BedZED is near London, England. But the development is like a small village. It has eighty-two houses and fourteen apartments. It also has workspace for one hundred people, a day care center, and an art center. It's near shops and public transportation.

BedZED opened in 2002. The fact that people live and work in this small village isn't unusual. What's special is how BedZED makes and uses energy.

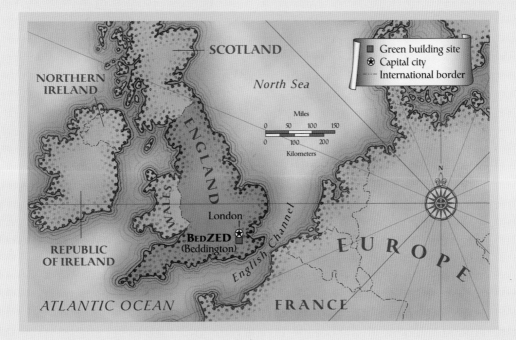

Above: *Oil rigs in Texas pump oil from under the ground, while oil rigs out at sea* (right) *tap into oil reserves under the ocean floor.*

ANCIENT ENERGY

Most of the energy we use comes from fossil fuels. Coal, natural gas, and petroleum (or crude oil) are all fossil fuels. Fossil fuels come from plants and animals that died millions of years ago. After the plants and animals died, their remains settled to the bottom of valleys, rivers, and seas. Over time, layers of dirt and rock piled up on the remains. Over millions of years, heat from Earth and the weight of dirt and rocks above changed the remains into coal, oil, and natural gas.

Miners dig up coal from underground. Drillers pump up oil and gas from underground and beneath the oceans. People burn fossil fuels to get energy.

CALCULATING YOUR *Carbon Footprint*

When you walk in the sand or snow, you leave footprints behind you. When you release carbon dioxide into the air, you are leaving a carbon footprint. Every person, family, business, and country leaves a carbon footprint. You can calculate your carbon footprint by using an online carbon calculator. The website Zerofootprint Kids Calculator (http://www .zerofootprintkids.com/ kids_home.aspx) has a carbon calculator just for kids.

Online carbon calculators ask you a series of questions: How many miles or kilometers does your family drive each year? How much and what kind of energy does your family home use? How many times do your family members fly on airplanes each year? The carbon calculator uses your answers to estimate your family's carbon footprint. In the United States, the average carbon footprint for a family of four is 7.5 tons (6.8 metric tons).

They use the energy to heat, cool, and light their homes and other buildings. Most cars also run on fossil fuel. They burn gasoline, which comes from petroleum.

WHAT'S WRONG WITH BURNING FOSSIL FUELS?

Fossil fuels produce lots of energy. But burning fossil fuels also hurts Earth and people. Burning fossil fuels causes air pollution. Air pollution can make people sick with lung cancer, asthma, and other serious diseases.

In addition, all fossil fuels contain carbon, a basic chemical. When burned, fossil fuels release their carbon in gas form. This gas, called carbon dioxide (CO_2), rises up in the atmosphere. The atmosphere is the layer of gases surrounding Earth. Because people have burned so much fossil fuel, the atmosphere holds more carbon dioxide than ever before.

All this carbon dioxide traps Earth's warmth. It causes temperatures on land to rise. This process is called global warming. Global warming has started to hurt Earth. Because of higher temperatures, ice is melting at the North Pole and South Pole. The melting ice has led to rising sea levels. Rising seas could flood islands and coastlines.

As Earth warms, some plants and animals won't survive. Global warming can also cause more extreme weather, such as floods, droughts, and hurricanes. To stop global warming, people must use less fossil fuel.

Fossil fuels take millions of years to form. People use up fossil fuels much faster than nature can replace them. If people continue digging up fossil fuels, Earth will eventually run out of its supply. People are looking for alternative fuels that will not harm Earth. People already use alternative fuels at BedZED.

CLEAN ENERGY DESIGN

Alternative fuels come from the sun, the wind, and other sources. Sun and wind are clean energy sources. They do not create pollution. In addition, no matter how much sun or wind power we use, we will never run out.

Designers of BedZED wanted to create buildings that used as little energy as possible. They wanted the energy to come from clean energy sources. At BedZED, solar panels collect the sun's energy. Other devices turn this energy into heat and electricity for buildings.

BedZED uses the sun in another way too. Most of the windows in the homes there face south. In the northern part of the world, the sun crosses the sky in the south. When the sun shines into south-facing windows, it gives extra warmth to homes.

BedZED has a centralized heat and power plant, called the CHP. The CHP does not rely on fossil fuels to make heat. Instead, it burns tree branch waste from local trees. When burned, the branches release carbon dioxide. But the CO_2 is offset, or absorbed, by the same trees the branches were cut from. The CHP uses the fuel to heat water. The heated water travels through pipes to BedZED's buildings. The pipes have thick insulation, or protective coverings, to keep the pipes hot. The hot pipes warm walls, floors, and rooms in BedZED's buildings.

"The Beddington Zero Energy Development . . . has been a flourishing green community since its conception in 2002."

—Kate Andrews, "BedZED: Beddington Zero Energy Development in London," 2008

Above: *Solar panels on BedZED's rooftops collect the sun's energy. Colorful vents that draw in the wind keep homes cool and deliver fresh air. Plants grown on rooftops continually absorb carbon dioxide, helping to clean the environment. Below left: Clean, modern apartments have south-facing windows to bring in natural light and warmth. Below right: BedZED has on-site recycling facilities and its own clean energy power plant.*

Drivers with electric cars can use outdoor outlets to charge their car batteries. BedZED is centrally located near buses and trains, making it easy for residents to use public transportation.

LOW-CARBON TRANSPORTATION

Most cars burn gasoline. They give off carbon dioxide and add to global warming. The amount of carbon dioxide that a vehicle or building releases is called its carbon emissions. BedZED's goal is to reduce carbon emissions from vehicle use by 50 percent.

To reach this goal, BedZED discourages its residents from using gasoline-powered cars. The development contains office spaces for one hundred workers. Some people who live in BedZED work in these offices. They can walk or ride bikes to work instead of driving cars. BedZED also has a day care center. Parents and children can walk or bike there too. The walkways around BedZED are well lighted, so people feel safe walking at night.

Not everyone works at BedZED. Some people must travel to jobs in London or another city. The community has organized carpools so that people can share rides to work. Some people at BedZED take buses and trains to work and school. By sharing cars and taking public transportation, people at BedZED cut down on pollution and carbon emissions.

BedZED has forty parking spaces for electric cars. The parking spaces have electric outlets. The electricity comes from BedZED's solar panels. People can plug in electric cars to recharge the batteries. Plug-in electric cars are not very common.

Eco-housing

An ecosystem is a community of living and nonliving things that support and depend on one another. For instance, in a forest ecosystem, some animals eat plants. They digest the plants and make dung, or waste. This waste eventually breaks down. It adds nutrients to the soil. Nutrients in the soil help plants grow. Animals eat the plants, and the cycle continues.

People who use green construction want to imitate the natural world. They want to create housing and other buildings that work in harmony with the surrounding ecosystem. People sometimes use the term *eco-housing* to refer to this kind of construction.

But many companies plan to sell these cars in the 2010s. When they do, the people at BedZED will be ready.

LIVING IN BEDZED

Living in BedZED is a lot like living in a regular house or apartment. The homes include bedrooms, sun lounges, living rooms, dining rooms, and kitchens. Some have outdoor patios, with private walkways and gardens.

On the inside, BedZED's houses and apartments look just like ordinary homes. But green building technology makes these homes much more energy efficient.

Left: *Natural light floods a BedZED home during the daytime.* Below: *Lots of people in this eco-village know their neighbors. BedZED residents share a sense of community.*

An enclosed porch in BedZED sports many flourishing plants. Many people in this green community like to tend their own small gardens.

BedZED makes it easy for residents to be environmentally friendly. All homes have lighting fixtures and appliances that don't use much energy. Homes also have built-in recycling bins for aluminum, glass, and other materials. When the bins are full, residents simply empty them at the BedZED recycling center.

BedZED homes offer comfort and style. Some people who live there are just as attracted to the beauty of the place as the environmental features. Many residents have become good friends. Their special green village has helped them form a bond.

"Green buildings are making giant strides now because of public debate and new technology."
—*Herbert Girardet, urban planner, 2007*

Residents enjoy little rooftop lawns and can grow their own vegetables and flowers if they wish. Bridges connect the buildings, enhancing the sense of community among the people who choose to call BedZED home.

THE FORD ROUGE CENTER'S *Living Roof*

In 2004 the Ford Motor Company reopened one of its oldest car factories. Called the Ford Rouge Center, the factory is in Dearborn, Michigan. The building has many green features. One of the most striking is its living roof.

Ordinary factory roofs are covered with shingles or metal. These hard surfaces allow rainwater to run off the rooftop quickly. Factory roofs are often coated in dirt and grime from the factory. When rain falls on an ordinary factory rooftop, the rainwater picks up dirt and pollution. The dirty water eventually flows into lakes and rivers.

Putting plants on rooftops instead of shingles or metal helps prevent this kind of pollution. The plants trap dust and dirt, so they don't wash away in the rain. And plants absorb carbon dioxide, which helps reduce a building's carbon footprint.

The Ford Rouge Center has the largest living roof in the world. It stretches across 10 acres (4.2 hectares). It is planted with sedum. This colorful, low-growing plant can survive even without much rainfall. Birds and insects make their homes in the sedum. Best of all, the living roof is constantly working to purify water and air.

CARBON SAVINGS

Despite its environmentally friendly features, BedZED still creates pollution. Some residents drive gasoline-powered cars. In addition, the CHP does not always work properly. When this happens, residents must use electric boilers powered by fossil fuels.

BedZED still puts carbon into the atmosphere, but it also takes carbon away. How do you get rid of carbon? Trees and other plants absorb carbon dioxide. Plants need carbon dioxide to live and grow. So people can offset their carbon emissions by planting trees and gardens.

The designers at BedZED have put gardens in interesting places— on the roofs of buildings. A garden on a rooftop is called a living roof. The living roofs at BedZED absorb carbon dioxide. They reduce the overall amount of carbon that BedZED releases into the air.

Because of its design, BedZED uses a lot less energy than other places. The houses use 88 percent less heat than other homes in the United Kingdom. People in BedZED drive cars 65 percent less than other British people. That is a big carbon savings.

2 Earthships

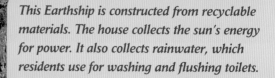

This Earthship is constructed from recyclable materials. The house collects the sun's energy for power. It also collects rainwater, which residents use for washing and flushing toilets.

*I*MAGINE YOU WERE GOING TO TAKE A LONG SEA VOYAGE. YOU WOULD HAVE TO MAKE SURE YOUR SHIP WAS STRONG ENOUGH TO WITHSTAND STORMS. YOU WOULD HAVE TO PACK EVERYTHING YOU NEEDED FOR THE TRIP, INCLUDING FRESHWATER AND FOOD. YOU MIGHT WANT SOME OF THE COMFORTS OF HOME, INCLUDING PLUMBING AND ELECTRICITY. WATER PIPES AND POWER LINES ON LAND WOULD NOT BE ABLE TO REACH YOUR SHIP TO PROVIDE THESE COMFORTS. YOU WOULD HAVE ONLY THE SUN, THE WIND, AND THE RAIN, AND THE ITEMS YOU PACKED AHEAD OF TIME.

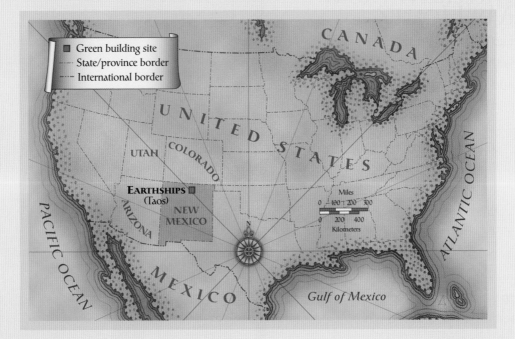

"The numbers of people continue to grow and the numbers of trees and sources of fuel continue to decrease."

—*Michael Reynolds*, Comfort in Any Climate, *2002*

New Mexico architect Mike Reynolds believes that homes on land should be like ships headed out for a long trip. The homes should be able to create their own energy and collect their own water. They should be made mostly from recycled materials or from things we already have on hand. And they should be easy to build. Since the 1970s, Reynolds has been building houses with all these qualities. He calls them Earthships.

HOW IS AN EARTHSHIP DIFFERENT FROM MY HOME?

Earthships provide their residents with energy, clean water, comfort, and protection from storms and earthquakes. That probably doesn't sound too different from the home you live in. The difference is that an Earthship doesn't rely on power plants, water treatment plants, or traditional building materials. Instead, an Earthship uses the sun to create its own energy. It harvests (collects) rainfall to get water. And builders make Earthships from natural and recycled materials—dirt, bottles, cans, and even tires.

Earthship architect Mike Reynolds leans against a bottle-brick wall in an Earthship modeled after his design.

Builders use tires, bottles, cans, and plain old dirt to make Earthships.

BUILDING AN EARTHSHIP

Building an Earthship is fairly simple. Some homeowners do most of the work themselves. Others hire people to build Earthships for them.

Builders use old car and truck tires to make the walls. They pack dirt inside the tires and stack them on top of one another. Builders then cover the walls with concrete or adobe. Adobe is a kind of clay.

Many people also decorate the walls with "little bricks." These bricks aren't made of clay like traditional bricks. Instead, they are empty bottles and cans. These containers reflect light and add color to the walls.

Mike Reynolds has created Earthships with many different floor plans. Some of the designs look similar to traditional homes. But most of them are very unusual.

Traditional houses usually have rectangular rooms and straight walls. Builders don't follow traditional rules when making Earthships.

One design looks like a castle. Another is shaped like a sea creature with a spiral shell.

Most people build Earthships against hillsides. A house built this way looks as if it's growing out of the side of the hill. The hill serves as a protective wall on one side of the house. It shields the house from cold and wind.

THE MANY BENEFITS OF USING OLD TIRES

Using tires to build walls makes good sense. Tires are strong and fireproof. When filled with dirt, tires are also solid and sturdy. And tires are made of rubber, a flexible material. This is a plus in places that have earthquakes.

HOTEL
Earthship

Want to see what it's like to live in an Earthship? Visit http:// www.earthship.net to learn more. People can even rent Earthships for the weekend.

TIRES THAT *Won't Go Away*

People in the United States get rid of 253 million old tires every year. Companies recycle about half of those tires. They use the rubber to make new products. The other tires pile up in landfills.

Tires do not decompose, or rot, naturally. Heat, cold, and water will eventually break down tires, but this might take thirty to one hundred years. A tire that is protected from the weather might last thirty thousand years. Building Earthships is a good way to recycle old tires so they don't sit for years and years in landfills.

During earthquakes, ordinary homes can fall down. Their rigid walls can crack and crumble. But the tires inside an Earthship move when the ground moves. So Earthships are not likely to fall apart during a quake.

Using old tires to make Earthships is an example of recycling. The tires have already been used on cars and trucks. People sometimes dump old worn-out tires in landfills. Sometimes you can see them piled in vacant lots. People who want to build Earthships can usually find old tires nearby. Unlike many traditional building materials, used tires don't need to be trucked long distances to a building site. This saves gasoline. An added bonus is that used tires are usually free.

CREATING AND STORING ENERGY

An Earthship uses the sun to create electricity. The roof of an Earthship has solar panels. These panels collect the sun's energy. Devices called photovoltaic cells turn the energy into electricity. Homeowners use this electricity to power all their electrical devices, including lights, computers, and television sets.

An Earthship also uses the sun's energy for heat. The front of the home is made up mostly of windows. In the Northern Hemisphere (the northern half of Earth), the windows face south to catch the sun. In the Southern Hemisphere, the windows face north to catch the sun.

Above: *Earthships capture the sun's energy with solar panels and south-facing windows.* Below: *Sun pours in through large south-facing windows to light the interior of this Earthship. In summer, residents draw the shades on south-facing windows to help keep the home cool.*

ON AND Off the Grid

Electricity is a form of energy. This natural force is all around us. Lightning is electrical energy. So is the shock you sometimes feel when you rub your stocking feet on carpet and then touch metal. That shock is called static electricity.

People have figured out how to create electricity using generators and other devices. From electrical generating stations, electricity travels through power lines and wires to homes and businesses. The system of power lines and wires that carries electricity is called the electric grid.

When a home or building is "off the grid," it does not rely on an electric station or power company for its electricity. Earthships are off the grid. They use solar panels and photovoltaic cells to create electricity. The energy comes from the sun.

When the sun's rays pour through the windows, the home's dense walls absorb the heat inside the house.

The thick dirt walls of an Earthship have a property called thermal mass. Thermal mass is the ability to store heat or cold. After an Earthship heats up, the thick walls hold the heat for a long time. They keep the inside of the house warm, even when the sun isn't shining. In winter it might be a bone-chilling 13°F (−11°C) outside. But inside the Earthship, it will be 64°F (18°C).

In summer, Earthship residents block out the sun's heat. They close the shades on their front windows. Remember that most Earthships are built against the sides of hills. Earth itself forms the rear wall of an Earthship. Earth has a great amount of thermal mass. It remains cool, even when the weather outside is hot. Earthships rely on this thermal mass for cooling. In summer the temperature outside might be a searing 100°F (38°C). But inside the Earthship, the temperature usually measures a cool 64°F (18°C).

"Building an Earthship costs as much as building an average size home, but without the utility [heat and electric] bills."

—Bianca Solorzano, CBS News correspondent, 2008

Earthships

Harvesting Water

Most of us think of harvesting crops, not water. But people can collect and store water just like crops. When rain falls onto the roof of an Earthship, the water collects in channels. The channels are a lot like gutters on a traditional home. But instead of carrying rainwater to the ground, the channels on an Earthship carry the rainwater into cisterns, or tanks. Pumps and gravity (Earth's downward pull) take the water through filters. The filters clean the water. They make it safe for drinking, cooking, and bathing.

Any water that's left over after cooking and washing drains into an interior botanical cell. The cell is a rubber-lined container. It holds gravel and plants. Some people plant fruit and vegetable gardens in their cells. But any plant will do. The plants naturally clean the water. The plant roots and the gravel filter the water and add bacteria. The good bacteria eats away harmful soaps and chemicals. Then residents can use the water again. Water that is too dirty for drinking or bathing goes to a separate drainage system. Residents use it as toilet water.

In general, Earthship residents use water collected from their rooftops four times over. The filtering ensures that residents always have a supply of clean water.

Rainwater travels from the roof into channels and then into cisterns.

Left: *Many people grow lush gardens inside their Earthships.* Right: *People around the world are discovering the benefits of Earthship living. This Earthship is in France.*

LIVING IN AN EARTHSHIP

People can build Earthships anywhere. They are suited to any climate, whether hot or cold. Most Earthships are in northern New Mexico, where Mike Reynolds started building them in the 1970s. But many other U.S. states have Earthships too. People have also built them in other parts of the world, including Europe, Australia, Central and South America, and Africa.

Why would anyone want to live in an Earthship? People living in ordinary homes use a lot of energy for heating, cooling, and lighting. A family living in an Earthship has a much smaller carbon footprint. People who live in Earthships say they feel good about working with the environment instead of hurting it.

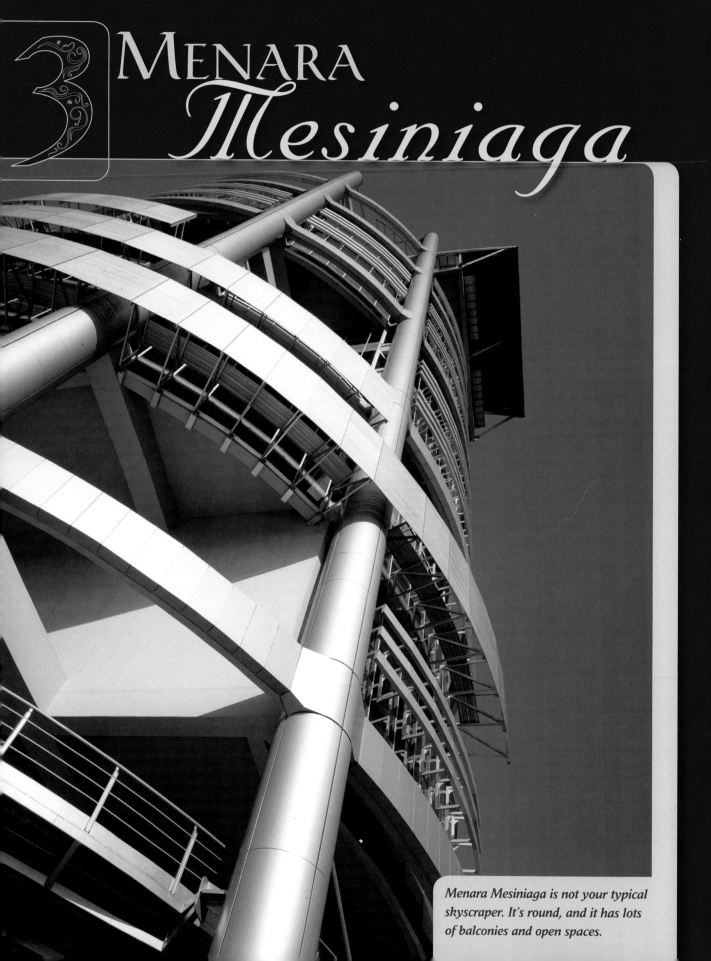

3 MENARA *Mesiniaga*

Menara Mesiniaga is not your typical skyscraper. It's round, and it has lots of balconies and open spaces.

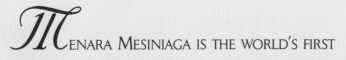

ENARA MESINIAGA IS THE WORLD'S FIRST GREEN SKYSCRAPER. THIS OFFICE BUILDING RISES ABOUT 150 FEET (300 M) IN DOWNTOWN KUALA LUMPUR, THE CAPITAL OF MALAYSIA. MALAYSIA IS A NATION IN SOUTHEAST ASIA. IT IS NEAR THE EQUATOR, THE IMAGINARY LINE THAT DIVIDES EARTH INTO NORTHERN AND SOUTHERN HALVES. PLACES NEAR THE EQUATOR HAVE HOT WEATHER ALL YEAR. THEY ALSO RECEIVE LOTS OF RAIN. THE REGION AROUND THE EQUATOR IS CALLED THE TROPICS. HOT, RAINY WEATHER IS CALLED TROPICAL WEATHER.

Kuala Lumpur has tropical weather. Temperatures there range from 70 to 90°F (21 to 32°C) year-round. The city is usually sunny in the daytime. The evenings are hot and sometimes have brief thunderstorms.

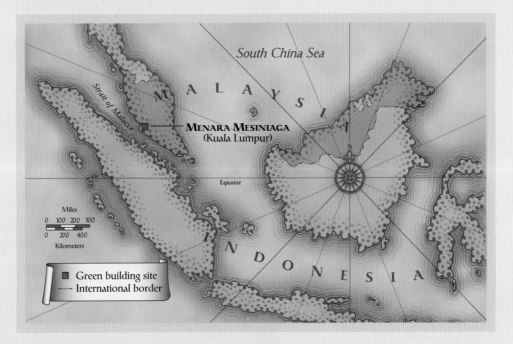

Malaysian architect Ken Yeang designed Menara Mesiniaga in the late 1980s. He wanted to create a skyscraper to fit Kuala Lumpur's tropical climate, or weather pattern. He also wanted to make a skyscraper that was good for the environment. His building uses plants, the sun, and the wind for lighting and cooling.

TRADITIONAL SKYSCRAPERS

Anyone who has visited New York City or Chicago, Illinois, has seen skyscrapers. These tall buildings provide spaces where many people can work or live. In big cities, land is expensive. People try to get as much usable space as they can from small plots of land. Skyscrapers take up very little space on the ground. But they can tower high into the sky. Each story, or level, is like another plot of ground.

Many modern skyscrapers look similar. They are tall, boxy towers made of steel, aluminum, concrete, and glass. These materials are strong. They can withstand fierce winds and cold weather. During winter the concrete in a skyscraper soaks up sunlight.

Architect Ken Yeang designs buildings that work with the environment.

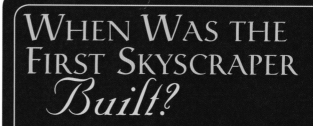

WHEN WAS THE FIRST SKYSCRAPER *Built?*

The first skyscraper ever built was the Home Insurance Building in Chicago. Builders took two years (from 1884 to 1885) to construct the skyscraper. This building was ten stories and 138 feet (42 meters) tall. It was one of the first buildings with a fireproof metal frame. The city tore it down in 1931 to make room for a new building.

Chicago (above) *was home to the world's first skyscraper. In modern times, the city is filled with many tall, boxy office towers.*

This absorption helps heat the building. In summer the steel and glass reflect some of the sunlight. This reflection helps keep the building from getting too hot. Traditional skyscrapers are well suited to cities such as Chicago and New York. These cities have cold, windy winters and hot summers.

Traditional skyscrapers have many windows. But people who work and live in the skyscrapers usually can't open the windows for a fresh breeze. Instead, they must rely on a skyscraper's air-conditioning system to keep them cool. When it's cold outside, people rely on the building's heating system to keep them warm.

"The skyscraper offers the greatest possibilities for [using] precious resources."

—Ken Yeang, architect, 2000

The Petronas Twin Towers rise high above the Kuala Lumpur skyline. Menara Mesiniaga is not nearly as tall, but it works in harmony with its tropical surroundings.

TROPICAL SKYSCRAPERS

Many skyscrapers in Kuala Lumpur look like the skyscrapers in New York. They have the same boxy design. These big buildings are impressive. They tell the world that the people who work there are successful and powerful.

But in a tropical city, a traditional skyscraper does not make sense. Its windows don't open to let in fresh tropical breezes. And the hot temperatures outside heat up the building's concrete year-round. In Kuala Lumpur, traditional skyscrapers must be air-conditioned constantly.

MALAYSIA'S SKYLINE

Kuala Lumpur is Malaysia's largest city. It has a tall skyline, with more than five hundred skyscrapers. Kuala Lumpur is home to the tallest twin buildings in the world. They are the Petronas Twin Towers. They reach 1,483 feet (452 m) into the sky. Each building has eighty-eight floors.

"*Yeang designs his buildings for . . . hot, humid [regions]. . . . For such climates and places one must start from scratch and think things anew.*"

—*Leland M. Roth*, Understanding Architecture, 2007

When designing Menara Mesiniaga, Ken Yeang wanted to take the climate into account. He wanted to use the tropical weather to heat and cool the skyscraper.

Menara Mesiniaga uses natural air-conditioning. Tropical breezes flow through its windows and open spaces.

AIR AND LIGHT

Workers built Menara Mesiniaga between December 1990 and December 1992. The design is elaborate. The building looks nothing like the boxlike skyscrapers of most cities. It is a complex, winding cylinder made of steel and aluminum. The outside walls contain many balconies and open spaces. This design gives Menara Mesiniaga a unique look and feel.

The building has many windows, and they open and close. It also has open spaces between floors. The windows and open spaces let natural breezes flow in and out of the building. People say that the tower can "breathe." The tower's many windows also allow sunshine to light the building during the daytime. These simple design features save a lot of electricity. Workers can do their jobs and be comfortable without turning on lots of lights or air-conditioning.

Menara Mesiniaga has special shutters that block the sun's powerful rays.

Windows facing the east and west have louvers. Louvers are similar to shutters. The louvers open and close to let in and block out sunlight. When the sun rises in the east and sets in the west, the louvers shade the windows from direct sunlight. This shade helps cool the building. It reduces the need for air-conditioning. Even the stairways and restrooms let in fresh breezes and sunlight.

GREEN GARDENS

Menara Mesiniaga has two large atriums, or inner courtyards. Native Malaysian plants grow inside the atriums. Some of the plants are tall trees and vines. They twist and wind up the atrium walls toward the roof and the balconies. A sunroof on top of the building provides the plants with light. The plants inside the tower provide natural shade. They help cool the building on hot days. The plants also improve air quality by releasing oxygen into the air. Clean air and fresh breezes are good for the health of people who work inside the tower.

BY ANY *Other* Name

"Menara Mesiniaga" means "Mesiniaga Tower" in the Malay language. Mesiniaga is the name of a Malaysian computer business. Mesiniaga partners with IBM, a big U.S. computer company. Because of this connection, Menara Mesiniaga is often called the IBM Tower.

Plants grow on balconies and in atriums (above). Inside, people take covered walkways (right) to their offices.

Menara Mesiniaga looks different than most other skyscrapers. And it provides a healthy and eco-friendly working environment.

Sick Building *Syndrome*

People often joke that going to school or work makes them sick. For some people, this complaint is no joke. People who study or work in airtight buildings sometimes feel sick inside them. These people may have sick building syndrome (SBS).

Several things can cause SBS. Chemicals used to make carpeting and furniture can make people sick. Mold, pollen, or viruses can also make people sick. These tiny organisms can breed wherever water collects in a building, including in humidifiers, carpeting, and ceiling tiles. In buildings that do not have good ventilation, or airflow, people can breathe in the harmful chemicals and organisms.

A person with SBS might suffer from headaches, a scratchy throat, watery eyes, a cough, dizziness, or fatigue. But the symptoms are often temporary. Once the person leaves the building, he or she usually feels well again.

People who design green buildings try to prevent SBS. They make sure the buildings have good ventilation. They include windows that open and close. Good ventilation means that people in a building are always getting a fresh supply of clean air.

Improving the Health of the Planet

Green skyscrapers such as Menara Mesiniaga work with the natural environment instead of against it. They require less electricity to light and cool the building than traditional skyscrapers do. And people who work in the buildings feel better in the healthier environment.

Ken Yeang believes that architects can and should create skyscrapers that are healthy for the people who live and work in them. He also thinks buildings should make use of their environment. For Yeang and other Malaysians, building a healthy building was a smart idea.

4 THE *Reichstag*

DEM DEUTSCHEN VOLKE

The historic Reichstag in Berlin, Germany, has been updated with state-of-the-art green technology.

ONE BUILDING IN GERMANY—THE REICHSTAG—

USES GREEN BUILDING TECHNOLOGY FROM TOP TO BOTTOM. THE

REICHSTAG IS GERMANY'S PARLIAMENT BUILDING. THE PEOPLE IN

PARLIAMENT ARE THE NATION'S LEGISLATORS, OR LAWMAKERS.

HISTORY OF THE REICHSTAG

The Reichstag has a long and rich history. The Germans built it between 1884 and 1894. The original building had a dome made of steel and glass. The dome was impressive. Many people considered it an architectural masterpiece.

When it was new, the Reichstag housed the government of the German Empire. In 1933 fire destroyed much of the building's interior, as well as most of the dome. The German parliament stopped meeting there. During World War II (1939–1945), enemy forces attacked Berlin. The attack damaged the Reichstag even more.

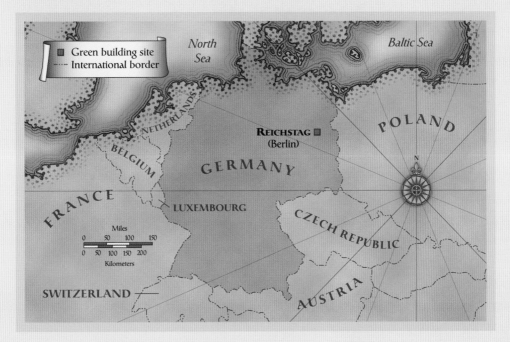

When creating the new Reichstag, Germans did not want to forget their history, including the damage to the building during World War II.

After the war, Germany became two countries. East Germany had one government. West Germany had another government. The Reichstag was in West Germany. But the building no longer housed the government. It sat empty. In the 1950s, West Germans repaired the building and removed its damaged dome. In the 1960s, they turned the building into a conference center, where groups could hold meetings.

On October 2, 1990, East and West Germany reunited as one country. The official ceremony took place at the Reichstag. Shortly afterward, German parliament members agreed to make the Reichstag their meeting place once again.

The Reichstag design, created by British architect Norman Foster (left), allows German citizens to see their lawmakers at work.

REDESIGNING THE REICHSTAG

Before the German parliament could meet at the Reichstag, the building needed to be repaired. In 1993 the German government held a contest to find the best design for the new Reichstag. Norman Foster, an architect from London, won the contest.

Foster's design focused on three goals. First, he wanted to make German citizens feel more connected to their government. He wanted them to be able to see members of parliament on the job. Second, he wanted to keep as much of the building's history as possible. Third, he wanted the building to help protect the environment.

To meet the first goal, Foster created one main entrance. Both parliament members and the public use this entrance. They can talk and share ideas as they walk in and out of the building together. On the first floor, Foster designed a big glass wall. It allows visitors to see hallways and parliament members inside the building. He also created a new glass dome in which people could walk around. When people in the dome look down, they can see legislators at work below. These features allow German citizens to see their government in action.

"The [dome allows] people to ascend symbolically above the heads of their elected representatives [in the chamber]."

——Foster + Partners, architects, 1999

Enemy armies occupied Berlin in 1945. Visitors to the Reichstag can read some of the graffiti that Russian soldiers wrote on the building's walls.

To preserve some of the building's history, Foster kept the original layout, or floor plan. He also kept the original outer walls and pillars. Some of them have graffiti, or writing and drawings, from World War II. Enemy soldiers scrawled the graffiti on the walls to insult the Germans. Foster kept the graffiti-covered pillars and walls as a piece of history.

THE DOME

The Reichstag's new dome also helps protect the environment. It is one of the building's most impressive features. The glass-walled dome measures 131 feet (40 m) across. It is 79 feet (24 m) tall and weighs about 1,200 tons (1,089 metric tons).

The dome contains two spiraling ramps. Visitors can walk up the ramps to an observation deck. From the observation deck, people can look through the glass walls and see the city of Berlin around them. They can also look down to see parliament members working below.

"The big glass lantern on top of the Reichstag sparkles with mirrored glass by day and is strobed by light at night, a sign that Berlin is once again the capital of a unified Germany."
—Nonie Niesewand, "Architecture: Norman's Berlin Conquest," 1999

Right: *Spiral ramps into the dome give visitors a view of government officials in session on the ground floor, as well as a full view of the city of Berlin. Below: When darkness falls, the dome lights up like a lantern.*

Left: *Members of Germany's parliament sit in the meeting chamber, which is lit from above by sunlight reflecting off the dome's mirrors.* Right: *Tourists get a look at the mirrored dome from the observation deck.*

In the center of the observation deck is a collection of 360 mirrors. Together, the mirrors form an upside-down cone. The cone is beautiful to look at, but it also serves an important purpose. When sunlight hits the cone, the mirrors reflect the light down into the chamber where parliament meets. During the day, the sun and the mirrors provide light for the chamber. This design saves energy, since people do not have to use electric lights in the chamber during the daytime.

INDOOR Sun

Architects often design buildings to take advantage of sunlight. Using natural light instead of artificial light is called daylighting. Daylighting reduces the amount of electricity a building uses.

SUNSCREEN FOR THE *Reichstag*

When direct sunlight bounces off a mirror, the light can hurt your eyes. Architect Norman Foster found a way to prevent this problem in the Reichstag dome. The dome has a movable shield. It keeps sunlight from hitting the mirrors directly. The shield follows the course of the sun. It moves along the mirrors throughout the day, blocking sunlight as necessary. A computer controls the shield's movements.

When it gets dark outside, parliament members must turn on the chamber's electric lights. The mirrors in the dome reflect the light shining up from below. The reflected light illuminates the dome. In this way, the dome becomes a lantern. When it lights up in the late afternoon, people outside the building know that parliament members are meeting inside.

As the sun moves through the sky, a shield follows its movements. The shield keeps direct sunlight from hitting the mirrors in the dome.

BELOW THE GROUND

The top of the building isn't the only environmentally friendly feature of the Reichstag. The building also has an underground power plant to make electricity. The plant does not burn fossil fuels. Instead, it runs on vegetable oil. Burning vegetable oil instead of fossil fuels reduces the Reichstag's carbon emissions by 94 percent.

Two aquifers also sit beneath the Reichstag. An aquifer is an underground layer of rock, sand, and gravel. This layer traps groundwater seeping down from above. One aquifer is 165 feet (50 m) below the Reichstag. The other is 984 feet (300 m) below. Water from the aquifers helps heat and cool the building.

The underground power plant creates a lot of heat when it makes electricity. The excess heat goes to the bottom aquifer. It makes the water in the aquifer extremely hot. The temperature reaches 158°F (70°C). When the building needs heat, pumps send the heated water up through pipes to the Reichstag. The heat from the water pipes warms the building.

The Reichstag uses the upper aquifer for cooling. Berlin can get cold in winter. The low temperatures cool the water in the upper aquifer to 41°F (5°C). Even in summer, the water remains very cool. People pump it up through pipes to cool the building, just as they pump up hot water to warm the building in winter.

Builders completed the Reichstag in 1999. Because of its history, its dome, and its environmental features, the Reichstag is one of Germany's top tourist destinations.

VEGETABLE *Energy*

The vegetable oil used in the Reichstag power plant comes from rapeseed. Rapeseed is a kind of herb. Germany harvests about 3.8 million tons (3.5 million metric tons) of rapeseed a year. Rapeseed oil is sometimes called canola oil.

When farmers grow rapeseed, the plants soak up carbon dioxide. The amount of carbon dioxide they absorb equals the amount released into the air when they are burned. The plants' carbon intake cancels out the carbon emissions.

The Reichstag's dome glows against the dark night sky.

5 7 WORLD TRADE CENTER

Finished in 2006, 7 World Trade Center is a tall glass building. It stands as a symbol that New York is rebuilding after terrorists attacked the United States in 2001.

On September 11, 2001, people in the United States faced a great tragedy. That morning, terrorists hijacked four passenger airplanes. The hijackers flew three of the planes into buildings. One plane hit and badly damaged the Pentagon. The Pentagon is the U.S. military headquarters near Washington, D.C. Two other airplanes flew into Tower 1 and Tower 2 (the Twin Towers) of the World Trade Center (WTC) in New York City. On the fourth airplane, passengers fought with the hijackers. The plane crashed in a field in Pennsylvania.

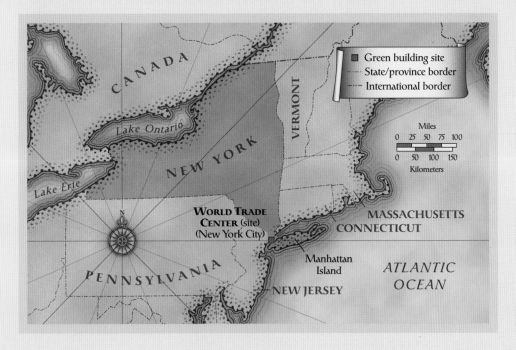

Glass, flames, and smoke burst out of the two World Trade Center towers after airplanes struck the skyscrapers in 2001.

The World Trade Center is a large business complex in New York City. People from all over the world come there to conduct business. Before the September 11 attacks, the WTC had seven buildings, including the Twin Towers.

The Twin Towers were two of the world's tallest skyscrapers. After the airplanes struck, the giant skyscrapers burned and collapsed. The fires, debris, and destruction from the Twin Towers caused a third WTC building to collapse. That building was the forty-seven-story Tower 7, or 7 World Trade Center (7 WTC).

Before the Twin Towers and 7 WTC fell, many people were able to leave the buildings. But some people couldn't get out in time. Altogether, about three thousand people died in the September 11 attacks. Most of them were trapped in the Twin Towers. The attacks on September 11 quickly became known as 9/11. Nine stands for September, the ninth month of the year. Eleven stands for the day of the attack.

FILLING AN EMPTY SPACE

After 9/11 New York City was left with a big empty spot and a large gap in the skyline. People wondered what to do with the space where the Twin Towers and 7 WTC had stood. Should the space be left empty as a memorial to all the people who died there? Should the city build a park in their honor? Or should people construct new buildings to replace the ones that had fallen?

In the end, New Yorkers decided to let the world know that the 9/11 attacks had not defeated their city but had made it stronger. They decided to build five new towers. The towers will be bigger and safer than the original WTC buildings. One building, Freedom Tower, or 1 World Trade Center, will be the tallest building in the United States. It will soar 1,776 feet (541 m) into the air. New Yorkers also decided to build a memorial park and a museum at the WTC site.

The Twin Towers site smoldered for days after the 9/11 attacks. New Yorkers decided to build new towers and a memorial to the people who died there.

An artist's model of the new World Trade Center site shows Freedom Tower on the far left and 7 WTC immediately to the right of Freedom Tower.

GREEN CERTIFIED

New Yorkers had another idea as well. Since they were building brand-new towers, why not use the newest technology to make the buildings green? People wanted the new towers to use less energy, produce less waste, and have cleaner indoor air than the original buildings did.

In 2002 builders put the plan into action. They started with 7 WTC. In 2006, after four years of construction, 7 WTC became the first of the new WTC towers to open its doors. It was also the first skyscraper in New York City to be green certified by the U.S. Green Building Council. To be green certified, 7 WTC had to meet many requirements. It had to:

- Reduce waste (by using recycled materials, for example)
- Save energy and water
- Be healthier and safer for people than traditional buildings
- Reduce carbon emissions

GREEN *Certified*

For an office building to be green certified by the U.S. Green Building Council, it must meet LEED requirements. LEED stands for Leadership in Energy and Environmental Design. The designers and builders of LEED-certified buildings must prove that their buildings are environmentally friendly.

THE MANY USES of Rainwater

People have been harvesting rainwater for thousands of years. In the ancient Middle East, farmers dug ditches to collect rainwater for their crops. The ancient Romans used rainwater to fill bathing pools inside their homes. The water from the pools also made houses cooler.

Collecting rainwater makes good sense. Rainwater can be used to water plants, flush toilets, and cool buildings. People can use filters and other devices to clean rainwater, making it safe to drink. And rainwater is free and easy to collect.

Collecting rainwater is also good for the environment. During heavy rainstorms, water can wash topsoil into rivers and streams. Plants need topsoil for its nutrients and to hold their roots in place. By collecting rainwater, people make sure that soil doesn't wash away in the rain. Heavy rains can also cause flooding. If enough people harvest rainwater, they can reduce floods.

RAINWATER HARVESTING

The rooftops of buildings are good places to harvest rainwater for future use. Gutters located on rooftops can channel water to large tanks at ground level or underground.

Designers included a rainwater harvesting system at 7 WTC. Some of the harvested rainwater travels through pipes to the grass and plants around the building. The rainwater also travels through pipes within the building's walls. On hot days, the water cools the building and reduces the need for air-conditioning.

Harvesting rainwater saves 7 WTC a lot of money on its water bill. The building uses about 30 percent less water than most other skyscrapers. That's a savings of about 1 million gallons (3.8 million liters) of water a year.

"We have reclaimed an important part of the downtown skyline, and in doing so, we have set new standards in environmental quality, life safety, and innovation."
—Larry Silverstein, World Trade Center developer, at the 7 WTC grand opening, 2006

OTHER ENVIRONMENTAL FEATURES

To save resources, the 7 WTC builders used recycled materials whenever possible. Thirty percent of the steel used to build the structure was recycled. It came from old buildings and other steel structures that had been torn down. Much of the wall insulation was also recycled.

The building has a lot of windows. During the day, instead of turning on electric lights, office workers rely on natural sunlight streaming through the windows. As the sunlight fades in the afternoon, the building's electric lights automatically get brighter. Working in natural sunlight makes people feel better, but some of the sun's rays can damage skin. So the 7 WTC windows are made from a special glass. It protects people from harmful rays from the sun.

Big walls of windows allow sunlight to pour into the top floor of 7 WTC.

SAFETY FIRST

The new 7 WTC is taller than the old one. It has fifty-two stories. It's stronger too. It has a steel structure. Its concrete walls are 2 feet (0.6 m) thick. Many of the construction materials are fireproof. If a fire does break out, the building is designed to keep it in one spot.

The builders did other things to increase safety. The stairwells are wider than they are in older skyscrapers. Wide stairwells allow a lot of people to use the stairs at the same time. During an emergency, office workers can exit quickly without crowding one another.

Many different companies rent office space in the tower. Workers appreciate the added safety features. But on a daily basis, some of the greatest benefits come from the building's green features.

New Yorkers held a special ceremony when 7 WTC opened in 2006. A group of schoolchildren sang at the ceremony.

6 JEAN-MARIE TJIBAOU
Cultural Center

The Jean-Marie Tjibaou Cultural Center in New Caledonia honors Kanak culture and traditional Kanak housing.

$\mathcal{N}$EW CALEDONIA IS A SMALL GROUP OF ISLANDS IN THE SOUTH PACIFIC OCEAN. THE ISLANDS ARE JUST EAST OF AUSTRALIA. SINCE 1853 NEW CALEDONIA HAS BEEN A FRENCH TERRITORY. FRANCE HAS SOME CONTROL OVER HOW NEW CALEDONIANS GOVERN THEIR ISLANDS.

About 250,000 people live on the islands. About 45 percent of them are native Pacific Islanders. They belong to an ethnic group called the Kanaks. The Kanaks have lived on the islands for thousands of years. About 34 percent of the people in New Caledonia are of French or other European ancestry. The rest of the islanders trace their ancestry to other places in Asia.

PAPUA NEW GUINEA

MELANESIA

FRENCH POLYNESIA

AUSTRALIA

NEW CALEDONIA ISLAND GROUP

JEAN-MARIE TJIBAOU CULTURAL CENTER (Nouméa)

SOUTH PACIFIC OCEAN

NEW ZEALAND

Miles
0 200 400 600 800
0 400 800 1200
Kilometers

N

■ Green building site

The cultural center is named after New Caledonia leader Jean-Marie Tjibaou (left), who was killed in 1989. Architect Renzo Piano (below) built the center to suit the tropical climate.

Mountains, pine trees, waterfalls, and white sandy beaches cover the islands. Lagoons and coral reefs lie offshore. Nouméa is the nation's capital city. It has many French restaurants and shops. The buildings in downtown Nouméa are mostly European-style buildings. The French built them during the 1800s and 1900s.

About 6 miles (10 kilometers) north of downtown sits the Jean-Marie Tjibaou Cultural Center. It is one of the most interesting structures in Nouméa.

THE CENTER

In 1989 an assassin killed Jean-Marie Tjibaou, New Caledonia's leader. Tjibaou was a Kanak. He wanted New Caledonia to be free of French rule. After Tjibaou's death, the French government wanted to honor Kanak culture.

The government hired Italian architect Renzo Piano to design a place to showcase Kanak history and the Kanak way of life. People chose the name Jean-Marie Tjibaou Cultural Center to honor the slain Kanak leader.

> *"Piano's architecture . . . is shaped not just by function and technology but also by the place and its traditions, and by an urge to settle into and integrate with the surroundings and nature."*
>
> —Peter Buchanan, Renzo Piano Building Workshop, 1999

Builders completed construction in 1998. The design blends modern building techniques with traditional Kanak architecture.

The center features ten wooden structures. Piano designed them to look like traditional Kanak great houses, or ceremonial houses. The tallest one is nine stories high. The houses are separated into three groups, called villages.

Built of tough iroko wood, the ten wooden structures can withstand fierce tropical storms.

Above: *This aerial photograph shows the wooden housing and the walkway connecting it.*
Below: *One of the gardens at the center grows banana trees and other native edible plants.*

Marie-Claude Tjibaou, Tjibaou's widow, walks through the gardens at the cultural center.

The center is a place where researchers can study Kanak culture. It includes an outdoor auditorium. It also has rooms for visiting artists, lecturers, scholars, and students.

Lush gardens surround the center. The gardens symbolize the history and culture of the Kanak people. According to Kanak mythology, the world began with only the sky, the moon, and the sea. One day the moon dropped a tooth into the sea. The tooth turned into worms, lizards, and other animals, including people. One garden at the cultural center has a pond with a rock in it. The rock symbolizes the dropped tooth and the birth of the Kanak people.

Another garden displays the plants that Kanak people traditionally used as medicines. It also has yams, bananas, cabbage, and taro. Kanak cooks commonly use these plants in cooking. A third garden displays plants that Kanaks typically grow near their homes. These include araucaria trees and coconut trees. A fourth garden has cordyline plants. When giving gifts to friends, family, or visitors, Kanaks place the items in the red leaves of this plant.

The gardens are symbols of Kanak culture. And the plants serve the environment. They absorb carbon dioxide, reducing the center's carbon footprint.

Jean-Marie Tjibaou Cultural Center

"The cultural center in Nouméa for the preservation of the Kanak culture by Renzo Piano represents a perfected masterpiece."

—*Werner Blaser*, Renzo Piano: Centre Kanak, 2001

BUILDING FOR THE WEATHER

When designing the cultural center, Renzo Piano considered its location. The center sits on the narrow Tina Peninsula. A peninsula is a piece of land surrounded by water on three sides. On one side of the cultural center lies the calm water of a lagoon. On the other sides are the Bay of Magenta, which merges with the rough waters of the Pacific Ocean. Piano also considered New Caledonia's tropical climate. The islands are generally warm and humid. Sometimes, cyclones, earthquakes, and tsunamis (tidal waves) hit the islands.

To help protect the center from violent weather, Piano built it from iroko wood.

The cultural center sits between a lagoon (below) *and the Pacific Ocean.*

STORM Warning

Cyclones are violent tropical windstorms. In North America, we call these storms hurricanes. Tsunamis are giant ocean waves. Undersea earthquakes often trigger tsunamis. In March 2003, a tropical cyclone pounded New Caledonia's west coast, including the Tina Peninsula. The storm's powerful winds tore off roofs, uprooted trees and crops, and knocked down power lines. The storm also killed two people, injured more than one hundred, and left about one thousand homeless. But because of their strong iroko wood walls, the buildings of the Jean-Marie Tjibaou Cultural Center remained unharmed.

A statue of Jean-Marie Tjibaou looks out over the cultural center.

This wood is very strong and durable. People sometimes use it to build boats. Iroko does not rot easily. It is hardy enough to withstand strong ocean winds.

Piano didn't just want to protect the buildings from ocean winds. He wanted to use the winds to cool the buildings. The great houses each have two layers of louvers. The outer louvers are made of wooden slats. After ocean winds filter through the slats, they reach the second layer of louvers. The inner louvers are made of glass. They automatically open or close, depending on the speed of the wind. The double louvers allow fresh air into the buildings. During violent storms, the louvers control how much wind enters the buildings. The louvers also force warm air upward toward the ceiling. This process helps cool the lower part of the buildings.

The cultural center is a tribute to the Kanak people in many ways. Through its design, it honors their culture and history. It also honors nature and the idea of living in harmony with the environment.

7 Samso

A wind turbine rotates on the Danish island of Samso. It provides electricity for the island's population.

SAMSO, AN ISLAND IN DENMARK, IS A CARBON-NEUTRAL SETTLEMENT. TO BE CARBON NEUTRAL, A PLACE MUST PRODUCE MORE CLEAN ENERGY THAN UNCLEAN ENERGY. THE CLEAN ENERGY CANCELS OUT THE UNCLEAN ENERGY, REDUCING THE CARBON FOOTPRINT TO ZERO.

For the people of Samso, becoming carbon neutral took some effort. But it was far easier than anyone on the island had imagined. Using wind turbines, solar panels, vegetable oil, and other tools, islanders took only five years to make Samso a green island.

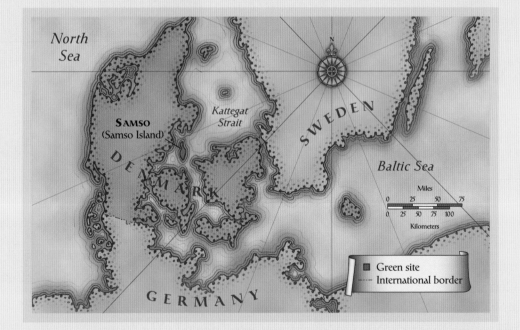

Above: *A quaint house stands on a street on Samso.*
Right: *Workers pick strawberries in the afternoon sun. Samsingers (people of Samso) showed that an entire community could go green.*

ABOUT SAMSO

Denmark is a nation in northwestern Europe. It consists of a mainland and many small islands, including Samso. Samso sits in the Kattegat Strait, which is part of the North Sea. West of the island is Denmark's mainland. East of the island lies the country of Sweden.

Samso is about 40 square miles (104 sq. km) in area. Its summers and winters are fairly mild. The average summer temperature is 68°F (20°C). The average winter temperature is about 32°F (0°C). The island has a population of just over four thousand year-round residents, known as Samsingers. Samsingers are famous for their strawberry and potato crops. But they are even more famous for creating the largest carbon-neutral settlement on Earth.

> "*[Soren] Hermansen showed up at every community or club meeting to give his pitch for going green.*"
>
> —Bryan Walsh, "Heroes of the Environment 2008," 2008

COMMUNITY INVOLVEMENT

In the late 1990s, the Danish government held a contest to see if an island could produce all its energy from local resources. The government wanted to know how islanders would heat their homes and businesses without coal and oil. How would they get electricity? The winners of the contest would have ten years to achieve their goals.

Soren Hermansen was an environmental studies teacher at a high school on Samso. He convinced Samsingers to enter the contest, and their plan won. The Danish government gave islanders some money to implement their plan. The rest was up to the community.

Soren Hermansen led the project to make Samso a carbon-neutral island.

After Samso won the contest, Hermansen met with community members. For the project to succeed, the people needed to work together. At meetings, islanders talked about their most valuable energy sources. These included sunshine, wind, straw, and rapeseed oil. Samsingers thought about how they could put these resources to work.

WIND AS ENERGY

People have been harnessing the wind's power for centuries. Farmers have long built windmills to turn pumps and other machines. Samso has strong winds along its coast. Samsingers knew they could use the power of wind to make energy.

Some of the Samsingers pooled their money to buy eleven wind turbines. Wind turbines are tall towers, 80 to 200 feet (24 to 61 m) high. They use the wind to generate electricity. After placing the turbines in three different spots on the island, islanders built a central plant to store the electricity.

Buying wind turbines turned out to be a good idea. The turbines generate enough electricity for the entire island. Islanders pay for the electricity they use, but it is cheaper than electricity from coal-burning plants. Some of the money Samsingers pay for electricity goes to repay the people who bought the turbines. Best of all, the turbines produce clean energy.

The wind turbines worked so well that islanders bought ten more of them. They placed the new turbines offshore—in the sea off the island's southern coast. With the original eleven turbines and the ten new ones, Samso generates more electricity than it needs. Islanders sell the extra electricity to people on the Danish mainland.

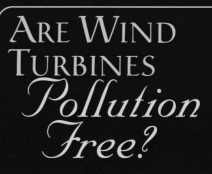

ARE WIND TURBINES *Pollution Free?*

The factories that built Samso's wind turbines most likely run on fossil fuels. They release carbon dioxide into the atmosphere. But when making energy, wind turbines themselves do not produce any carbon dioxide or other pollutants.

Above: *A farmer sits high above his fields while showing off one of his wind turbines.* Below: *A row of ten wind turbines lines the shores of Samso. The turbines turn wind energy into electricity.*

STRAW, SUN, AND SHEEP

Samsingers didn't stop with the wind. Instead of burning oil or gas to power their home furnaces, islanders use straw. Straw consists of dried stalks of grain, such as wheat and rye. Straw and other plants used as fuel are called biofuel.

Farmers on the island grow the wheat and other grain that makes the straw. Samsingers then burn the straw in three heating plants. Underground pipes carry the heat to homes and other buildings.

Burning straw releases carbon dioxide into the air. But when farmers plant a new field of crops to get more straw, the new plants absorb the extra carbon dioxide. By producing carbon but then taking it away, Samsingers are able to reduce their carbon footprint.

Instead of fueling cars and tractors with gas, Samsingers use rapeseed oil. This vegetable oil comes from rapeseed, a crop that grows well on the island. Finally, Samsingers have placed solar panels on rooftops and in fields to collect the sun's energy. Sheep graze on the fields' grasses. They keep the grass from growing tall and covering the solar panels. About 70 percent of the island's heat comes from solar energy.

> *"I've just been to the [United States] . . . they could make a lot of energy with all that sunshine."*
>
> —*Erik Koch Andersen, Samso resident, 2007*

AN ENVIRONMENTAL MODEL

By 2003 Samso was carbon neutral. But islanders still create some pollution. To reach the mainland from Samso, people must take ferries. Ferries run on fossil fuels. In addition, Samsingers' household items, clothes, wind turbines, and solar panels come from factories that create pollution. But Samsingers are still carbon neutral because they produce more clean energy than they use. The energy they make balances out the pollution.

By working together, Samsingers have made a positive difference in their environment. People on the island benefit by earning money from the electricity they generate. And they accomplished their clean-energy goals in half the time allowed. Samso has become an environmental model for the rest of the world.

Rows of solar panels in a field on Samso capture the sun's energy.

TIMELINE

1933	Fire destroys much of the interior of the Reichstag, Germany's parliament building.
1945	Enemy forces write graffiti on the Reichstag's walls.
1970s	Mike Reynolds starts building Earthships in New Mexico.
late-1980s	Ken Yeang begins designing the Menara Mesiniaga in Malaysia.
1989	Jean-Marie Tjibaou, Kanak president of New Caledonian provisional government, is assassinated.
1990	East and West Germany reunite as one country (Germany).
1992	Workers complete Menara Mesiniaga.
1993	The German government holds a contest to choose a new design for the Reichstag.
1998	Workers complete the Jean-Marie Tjibaou Cultural Center. Samsingers begin their project to make Samso a carbon-neutral island.
1999	Builders complete the new Reichstag.
2000	Builders begin work on BedZED in England.
2001	On September 11, terrorists attack the Pentagon and the World Trade Center in the United States.
2002	Workers start rebuilding 7 World Trade Center. BedZED opens its doors to residents.
2003	Samso achieves its goal of becoming a carbon-neutral island.
2004	The Ford Motor Company creates the world's largest living roof at the Ford Rouge Center.
2006	The first green-certified office tower in New York City, 7 WTC, reopens.
2009	Companies began to sell several models of plug-in electric cars.
2012	Freedom Tower is scheduled to open.

CHOOSE AN EIGHTH WONDER

Now that you've read about the Seven Wonders of Green Building Technology, do a little research to choose an eighth wonder. You may enjoy working with a friend.

To start your research, look at some of the websites and books listed on the following pages. Use the Internet and library books to find more information. What other structures or places use green building technology? Think about buildings and communities that

- *Reduce carbon emissions*
- *Use recycled materials*
- *Save energy and water*

You might even try gathering photos and writing your own chapter on the eighth wonder.

8

GLOSSARY AND PRONUNCIATION GUIDE

aquifer (AHK-weh-fur): an underground layer of rock, sand, or gravel that holds freshwater

architect: a person who designs buildings and advises builders on their construction

atmosphere: the layer of gases surrounding Earth or another body in space

biofuel: fuel made from recently dead plants

carbon dioxide (KAHR-behn deye-AHK-seyed): a colorless, odorless gas. Extra carbon dioxide in the atmosphere is leading to global warming.

carbon footprint: the amount of carbon that a person, family, building, or organization releases into the atmosphere each year

carbon neutral: producing more clean energy than unclean energy

climate: the typical weather patterns found in a region

fossil fuels: fuels formed millions of years ago from the remains of dead plants and animals. Coal, gas, and petroleum are all fossil fuels.

generator: a machine that turns mechanical energy into electrical energy

global warming: an increase in the average temperatures on Earth

louver (LOO-vur): a window covering with movable slats. Louvers can be opened or closed to let in or block out wind, light, and rain.

photovoltaic (foh-toh-vahl-TAY-ihk) cells: devices that turn solar energy into electrical energy; also called solar cells

recycle: to use materials over again instead of throwing them away

solar panels: devices that collect the sun's energy for conversion into heat or electricity

technology: tools and techniques that people use to make and do things

thermal mass: the ability of a substance to absorb and store heat or cold

tropics: regions near the equator. Tropical regions are hot year-round and often very rainy.

wind turbine: a machine that changes the power of rushing wind into electrical energy

SOURCE NOTES

10 Kate Andrews, "BedZED: Beddington Zero Energy Development in London," Inhabitat, January 17, 2008, http://www.inhabitat.com/2008/01/17/bedzed-beddington-zero-energy-development-london/ (March 30, 2009).

15 Herbert Girardet, quoted in Michelle Jana Chan, "Building the Future," CNN.com, October 31, 2007, http://edition.cnn.com/2007/TECH/10/31/fs.greenbuild/ (March 30, 2009).

20 Michael Reynolds, *Comfort in Any Climate* (Taos, NM: Solar Survival Architecture, 2000), 2.

25 CBS News, "Living Green in Earthships," CBS News, October 9, 2008, http://www.cbsnews.com/stories/2008/10/09/earlyshow/main4511601.shtml (March 30, 2009).

31 Ken Yeang, *The Green Skyscraper: The Basis for Designing Sustainable Intensive Buildings* (New York: Prestel, 2000), 19.

33 Leland M. Roth, *Understanding Architecture: Its Elements, History, and Meaning* (Boulder, CO: Westview Press, 2007), 609.

41 Foster + Partners, "The Plenary Building in a Converted Reichstag," Foster + Partners, April 19, 1999, http://www.fosterpluspartners.com/News/017/Default.aspx (June 11, 2009).

42 Nonie Niesewand, "Architecture: Norman's Berlin Conquest," *Independent*, April 19, 1999, http://www.independent.co.uk/arts-entertainment/architecture-normans-berlin-conquest-1088321.html (July 15, 2009).

53 Lower Manhattan Construction Command Center, "7 World Trade Center Opens with Musical Fanfare," Lower Manhattan.info, May 22, 2006, http://www.lowermanhattan.info/news/7_world_trade_center_50451.aspx (July 5, 2009).

54 Jackie Cravern, "The New York World Trade Center," About.com, n.d., http://architecture.about.com/od/worldtradecenter/ss/worldtrade.htm (March 31, 2009).

59 Peter Buchanan, *Renzo Piano Building Workshop*, vol. 1 (New York: Phaidon Press, 1999), 3–4.

61 Werner Blaser, *Renzo Piano: Centre Kanak* (Basel, Switzerland: Birkhauser, 2001), 15.

67 Bryan Walsh, "Heroes of the Environment 2008: Soren Hermansen," *Time*, 2008, http://www.time.com/time/specials/packages/article/0,28804,1841778_1841782_1841789,00.html (March 31, 2009).

71 Samso Energy Academy, "Erik Koch Andersen," Samso Energy Academy, June 19, 2007, http://www.energiakademiet.dk/front_uk.asp?id=46 (March 31, 2009).

SELECTED BIBLIOGRAPHY

Andrews, Kate. "BedZED: Beddington Zero Energy Development in London." Inhabitat, January 17, 2008. http://www.inhabitat.com/2008/01/17/bedzed-beddington-zero-energy-development-london/ (July 15, 2009).

Earthship Biotecture. "Earthship Biotecture: Sustainable, Independent Buildings and Systems." Earthship Biotecture. 2009. http://www.earthship.net/ (July 15, 2009).

Esty, Daniel C., and Andrew S. Wintson. *Green to Gold: How Smart Companies Use Environmental Strategy to Innovate, Create Value, and Build Competitive Advantage.* New Haven, CT: Yale University Press, 2006.

GHC Bulletin. "Geothermal Pipeline: Progress and Development Update from the Geothermal Progress Monitor." *GHC Bulletin,* 2000. http://geoheat.oit.edu/bulletin/bull21-4/art7.pdf (July 15, 2009).

Jencks, Charles. *The New Paradigm in Architecture: The Language of Post-modernism.* New Haven, CT: Yale University Press, 2002.

McKie, Robin. "Isle of Plenty." *Observer,* September 21, 2008. http://www.guardian.co.uk/environment/2008/sep/21/renewableenergy.alternativeenergy (July 15, 2009).

McNamara, Melissa. "Danish Island Is Energy Self-Sufficient." CBS Interactive. 2007. http://www.cbsnews.com/stories/2007/03/08/eveningnews/main2549273.shtml (July 15, 2009)

Niesewand, Nonie. "Architecture: Norman's Berlin Conquest." *Independent,* April 19, 1999. http://www.independent.co.uk/arts-entertainment/architecture-normans-berlin-conquest-1088321.html (July 15, 2009).

Philips, Derek, and Carl Garner. *Daylighting: Natural Light in Architecture.* Burlington, MA: Elsevier, 2004.

Reynolds, Michael. *Comfort in Any Climate.* Taos, NM: Solar Survival Architecture, 2000.

Walsh, Bryan. "Heroes of the Environment 2008: Soren Hermansen." *Time.* 2008. http://www.time.com/time/specials/packages/article/0,28804,1841778_1841782_1841789,00.html (July 15, 2009).

Yeang, Ken. *The Green Skyscraper: The Basis for Designing Sustainable Intensive Buildings.* New York: Prestel, 2000.

FURTHER READING AND WEBSITES

Doeden, Matt. *Green Energy: Crucial Gains or Economic Strains?* Minneapolis: Twenty-First Century Books, 2010. This entry in the USA TODAY'S Debate series explores the pros and cons of investing money and resources into green technology.

Fridell, Ron. *Earth-Friendly Energy*. Minneapolis: Lerner Publications Company, 2009. Fridell describes how people obtain and use renewable energy in the forms of wind, solar, water, and geothermal power.

Parker, Steve, and Laura Buller. *Electricity*. New York: DK Children, 2005. In this book you'll learn about electricity and how it works.

Silverstein, Alvin, Virginia Silverstein, and Laura Silverstein Nunn. *Energy*. Minneapolis: Twenty-First Century Books, 2009. This book describes all types of energy and how people use it. It also discusses the effect of energy use on the environment and talks about future energy sources.

———. *Global Warming*. Minneapolis: Twenty-First Century Books, 2009. This title takes a close look at how humans are changing Earth's climate.

Walker, Niki. *Harnessing Power from the Sun*. New York: Crabtree Publishing, 2007. This book explains in detail how solar energy is replacing fossil fuels. The book describes solar panels, solar cells, and other devices.

Welsbacher, Anne. *Earth-Friendly Design*. Minneapolis: Lerner Publications Company, 2009. The author explains how people are changing the ways they live, travel, and produce goods to be more Earth friendly.

Websites

Earthship Biotecture
http://www.earthship.net/web/
On this website, you'll learn more about Earthships and how they produce their own energy.

Energy Kid's Page
http://www.eia.doe.gov/kids/energyfacts/sources/renewable/solar.html
This site makes it fun and easy to learn how the sun produces energy.

How Wind Turbines Work
http://www1.eere.energy.gov/windandhydro/wind_how.html#inside
On this site from the U.S. Department of Energy, you can click on a diagram of a wind turbine and see it in action.

Samsø Energy Academy
http://www.energiakademiet.dk/default_uk.asp
Read articles and learn more about Samso's environmental efforts and its people. Some of the information is in Danish. But most of the site is in English.

Zerofootprint Kids Calculator
http://www.zerofootprintkids.com/kids_home.aspx
This fun website helps kids determine their carbon footprints.

INDEX

ABOUT THE AUTHOR

Karen Sirvaitis is a freelance writer and editor. She has written more than twenty books. She lives in northwestern Wisconsin with her family.

PHOTO ACKNOWLEDGMENTS